The PERSONAL COOKBOOK

by
Wendy Baker

LONGMEADOW
PRESS

THE PERSONAL COOKBOOK
was produced and prepared by
Quarto Marketing Ltd.
15 West 26th Street
New York, NY 10010

Cover Design: Liz Trovato
Illustrations: Susan Paradis

Typeset by BPE Graphics, Inc.
Printed and bound in Hong Kong by Leefung-Asco Printers Ltd.

Exclusive for Waldenbook Co.

C O N T E N T S

PART IV
The Recipe Recordkeeper

HORS D'OEUVRE AND APPETIZERS
PAGE 44

SALADS
PAGE 52

SOUPS AND STOCKS
PAGE 58

PASTA AND RICES
PAGE 64

EGGS
PAGE 70

VEGETABLES
PAGE 74

SAUCES, DRESSINGS, AND STUFFINGS
PAGE 80

FISH
PAGE 86

POULTRY AND GAMEBIRDS
PAGE 92

MEAT
PAGE 100

BREADS
PAGE 110

PIES, PASTRIES, CAKES, AND COOKIES
PAGE 116

ICINGS, CANDIES, TOPPINGS, AND GLAZES
PAGE 124

PUDDINGS, MOUSSES, AND FRUITS
PAGE 128

JELLIES AND PRESERVES
PAGE 132

PICKLES AND RELISHES
PAGE 136

BEVERAGES
PAGE 140

PART I
Basic Information

STANDARD COOKING TECHNIQUES

BAKING

Baking is cooking food by dry heat. Preheat your oven 12–20 minutes at the desired temperature before inserting food and use an oven thermometer to check the temperature. Do not crowd pans and dishes into the oven or place one directly below the other; alternate their positions on the shelves so the air can circulate around them freely.

Baking at an elevation of 3,000 feet or more requires adjusting your recipe. The ingredients affected are the baking powder and soda, which quickly produce gas and cause quick breads to collapse. Decrease their amounts by one fourth.

Yeast bread has an even stronger reaction to the high elevation. It will rise at an accelerated rate, so punch it down and let it rise again to double its bulk. Also use a little *less* yeast and a little *more* water.

Popovers pop up almost instantly. Add another egg to the batter to strengthen their shells.

Cake is the most sensitive to heights. It is likely to fall and become coarse-textured unless you modify your recipe. But first generously grease and flour-dust the cake pan; cakes tend to stick to surfaces easily above 3,000 feet.

At 3,000 to 5,000 feet, reduce each teaspoon of baking powder by ⅛ teaspoon, reduce each cup of sugar by 3 teaspoons, and increase each cup of liquid by 2 to 4 tablespoons.

At 5,000 to 7,000 feet, reduce each teaspoon of baking powder by ⅛ to ¼ teaspoon, reduce each cup of sugar by 2 tablespoons, and increase each cup of liquid by 2 to 4 tablespoons.

At 7,000 to 10,000 feet, reduce each teaspoon of baking powder by ¼ teaspoon, reduce each cup of sugar by 1 to 3 tablespoons, and increase each cup of liquid by 3 to 4 tablespoons for best results.

Above 10,000 feet, reduce each teaspoon of baking powder by ¼ to ½ teaspoon, reduce each cup of sugar by 2 to 3 tablespoons, add an extra egg to the batter, and increase each cup of flour by 1 to 2 tablespoons.

BLANCHING

There are several meanings for the word blanching. It can mean pouring boiling water over food to crack its skin and make peeling easier, as with tomatoes and peaches. It also refers to plunging food into a large pot of boiling water a little at a time so the boiling continues, then cooking for the required length of time. It is then plunged into cold water, drained, and stored. Another method is to plunge vegetables into boiling water just long enough to stop enzyme action, then into cold water and store. Steam blanching is suspending food in a wire basket above boiling water in a covered kettle. When the steam begins to escape from under the lid, start timing and cook as directed on the cooking instructions. The latter three methods are used prior to canning and freezing vegetables because they preserve color and prevent deterioration.

BOILING

As common as it is to hear "bring to a boil," food does not benefit from prolonged boiling and it should be done only in specific circumstances. Adding foods to boiling water, such as pasta, rice, cooked cereals, potatoes, frozen vegetables, is necessary for them to cook properly. But once the food has been added, the temperature of the water lowers and should remain simmering thereafter. Even boiled eggs should be simmered. It is a good rule of thumb for soups, stews, sauces, and vegetables not to boil for any length of time to preserve their original food values.

BROILING

To broil something is to cook it under strong direct heat one side at a time. There is no need to preheat a broiler, particularly if it's below the oven. In fact it is a waste of fuel because the food is not cooked by the heat of the compartment, but by the flames themselves.

If the meat you are cooking is very lean, remove the rack and grease it with vegetable oil or meat fat. Then reinsert it 3 inches below the flame. A very thick piece needs to be lower or else the outside will get overdone before the inside is cooked. Score the edges of the meat to keep them from curling up while cooking.

Cook briefly on one side, turn, and cook for a half of the total time required (see Cooking Temperatures and Times), turn again to complete. Meat has reached medium stage when drops of pink juice show on the surface, and when pressed, it feels neither soft nor hard. Thin pieces of fish should not be turned at all. When meat is nearly done, remove and season with salt and pepper, and place on a carving board with a piece of foil covering it. It will finish cooking in its own heat.

Cleaning the broiler pan will be easier if you sprinkle it with salt or detergent and cover it with paper towels.

CASSEROLE COOKING

Cooking complementary foods together in an ovenproof dish is called casseroling. The ingredients are usually a combination of noodles, rice, or potatoes; meat or fish; vegetables; and a cream or cheese sauce or broth. Wines and liqueurs can also lend interest to casseroles, as do fresh herbs.

The advantages of casseroling are being able to prepare everything ahead of time and using convenience food, for example, canned fish, frozen vegetables, and condensed soups. If you do a lot of casseroling, it is worthwhile to keep basic supplies on hand. Frozen chopped onions and green peppers do not lose their flavor; chicken stock base, canned condensed cream of mushroom and cream of celery soups keep on the shelf for a long time; and for toppings grated parmesan cheese and slivered almonds both keep well in the refrigerator.

The ovenproof casserole dish should be cleaned before and after cooking so any stains or spills will not darken and become part of the dish. Casseroles should be cooked uncovered or too much steam will develop and ruin the sauce. Cooking times and oven temperatures will depend, to some extent, on what the casserole dish is made of, its size and shape, and the depth of food in it. Glassware absorbs heat quickly, so reduce temperature by 25 degrees. A casserole made in a deep earthenware dish will need to be cooked longer than the same casserole made in a shallow dish. Use times and temperatures given for recipes as a guide. Check your casserole as it's cooking. A casserole made in a long, shallow dish is better for large groups of people because the heat will spread evenly.

DEEP-FAT FRYING

Choose a heavy saucepan or kettle with a flat bottom and short handles. Using shortening, vegetable or peanut oil (never olive oil), fill it half full. There should always be enough oil to completely cover the food and let it move around; yet there should be enough air space left in the pan for the oil to bubble up.

Heat the oil gradually. To judge the temperature of the fat, use a frying thermometer or the bread cube test. Drop a bread cube into the oil and count to 60. If the bread turns brown in 1 minute, the temperature is approximately 365 degrees Fahrenheit, which is the normal deep-fat frying temperature.

The oil must be hot enough so the food doesn't absorb it, but not smoking. If it starts to smoke, discard the oil and start again. Smoking indicates the oil is breaking down. It will burn the outside of the food, leaving the inside raw.

A wire basket is a must for deep-fat frying potatoes, onions, eggplant, clams, etc. Also keep on hand metal tongs, a slotted spoon, and, for draining the cooked food, a stack of paper towels.

The food going into the fry pan should be dry, so as not to splatter, and room temperature. Add it a little at a time so the temperature of the oil doesn't drop.

After frying a batch, let the temperature return to normal and skim out any particles of food.

The oil may be used again by adding raw potato slices, which will absorb the food flavor. Scoop out the potatoes, strain the oil through cheesecloth, and store. When the oil becomes dark and cloudy it is not suitable for reuse.

DOUBLE BOILER COOKING

Foods such as chocolate sauce, which can be ruined when overheated, will benefit from being cooked in a double boiler. A wide pan is easier for stirring and making sure the sauce is evenly heated. If you are cooking many dishes at once, begin the sauce directly over the heat and then once it's on its way, transfer it over the pot of hot water.

FLAMBÉING

Flambéing is a dramatic touch that, if safely performed, will enliven any dinner party and thrill your guests. The points to remember for a successful flambé are the following:

The food that is to be inflamed must be warm and so should the brandy or liqueur. Heat the liqueur gently under a warm flame. When it's very warm, but well under the boiling point, tilt the brandy slowly from the pan into the serving dish. With meat, do not use less than 1 ounce of liqueur per serving. Apply the lighted match close to the surface of the brandy at the edge of the dish and be careful not to lean over it. It should ignite immediately in a running blue flame. Serve when the flame disappears. For hot desserts, sprinkle the surface with granulated sugar before adding the warmed liqueur. Then ignite. For flaming puddings, soak sugar cubes in orange or lemon extract, place them on the pudding, and ignite.

PAN FRYING

First dredge the food in a coating of seasoned flour, bread crumbs, or corn meal. In a heavy pan heat a little oil or, if you are pan frying meat, melt a little fat trimmed off the meat over medium heat. Cook one side at a time until it becomes golden brown and, with meat, juices appear on the surface. Turn and repeat. Drain the food on paper towels and serve immediately.

PLANKING

Planking, although somewhat unusual, is a delicious method of cooking and serving meat. It entails broiling a steak on a slab of wood usually made of oak and about one-inch thick. The board acts as a flavor-enhancer, making the meat taste as though it were cooked over an open fire in the woods. Planks often have a design of a tree carved into their surface to collect the meat juices, which you can pour over the cooked steak.

To keep it from charring, an unused plank must be seasoned first. Brush it with vegetable oil and heat it for 1 hour in a 225-degree oven. Just before cooking the meat, trim off the fat and place it on the uncovered plank. Put the board in the oven for 10 minutes until it is saturated with the melted fat. Now broil the steak by itself on one side. When it is nicely browned put it on the plank, cooked side down, and broil the other side. The steak may be served from the plank.

POACHING

The principle of poaching is cooking food in a liquid that is kept just below boiling and which acts as a basting. The liquid is not deep enough to cover the food, but when the pan is covered the steam bastes the top. An egg, properly poached, is cooked this way. However, fish and other delicate food that take longer to cook than eggs can become trapped in too much steam. Hence, leave the lid off the pan and baste the food or cover it loosely with foil.

Fish tastes exceptionally delicious when poached in dry white wine or vegetable stock. If you have insufficient stock, add cream or wine. Vinegar added to the water when poaching will keep the white of an egg from running (1 teaspoon vinegar to 4 cups water). When poaching a whole chicken, the water is put on cold, the chicken added to the pot, and then the water brought to a simmer.

PRESSURE COOKING

A pressure cooker captures steam, causing it to rise well above the boiling point and forcing it through the food. Cooking times are reduced considerably because of the intense heat. Only a small amount of liquid is needed to produce the steam. *Be sure to carefully follow the manufacturer's directions for your pressure cooker.*

Vegetables or other solids should fill two thirds of the cooker; liquids not more than half. Season lightly because spices are not diluted by the steam. Break up bones as small as possible. Meat, poultry, and game should have all the fat trimmed off. It is crucial that meat not be overcooked because the protein fibers get hard and stringy. Pot roast and chicken usually take 10–12 minutes per pound. Large pieces (over 3 pounds) get overcooked on the outside before they're done on the inside. Foods that should never be cooked in a pressure cooker are split peas, cranberries, pasta, and applesauce for they will splatter, clogging the vent.

If you are cooking foods with different cooking times, start with whatever takes the longest, adding the other ingredients in their cooking-time order. Remember to reduce pressure before opening the lid. Begin timing your food in the pressure cooker from the minute you cap the vent. Always be sure to release the air in the cooker before capping it. After cooking wait for the pressure to subside before removing the lid. (The hissing will stop.) Running cold water over the pot will hasten this.

REDUCING

The most important step in sauce making, reducing is boiling down a liquid to intensify its taste. A wine or broth sauce are examples of reduced liquids. Sauces with eggs cannot be reduced, of course, and those with a flour base must be constantly watched and stirred continuously in order to avoid scorching.

SAUTÉING

Sauté in a heavy frying pan or any heavy pan with low sides. A high-sided pan will cause the food to steam instead of sear because the food's moisture can't evaporate quickly. This is a rapid process, with the heat kept high and the food cut small. Use fat, oil, or butter plus oil. Butter by itself won't become hot enough without burning, hence it should be clarified or fortified with oil (1 tablespoon to every 2–3 tablespoons butter).

Food must be dry before putting it in the pan and enough space must be left between each piece of food or it will not brown. To keep it from overbrowning, agitate the pan. Too much turning of the food interferes with the fast heating.

SCALDING

Usually in reference to milk, scalding means cooking at just below the boiling point at a temperature of 185 degrees: when something has reached that point tiny bubbles form around the edge of the pan. Heating is done either over direct heat or in the top of a double boiler.

SIMMERING

Simmering food is such a gentle process that the bubbles barely break when they reach the surface of the water. It is a very important method of heating food because it miraculously protects delicate foods and yet softens tough ones. It should be used for braises, soups, stews, fricassees, eggs, and sauces. Cover the lid on the pans except for soups.

SKEWERING

Skewer cooking done indoors is either broiled, baked, or braised. Outdoors, food is grilled over a fire. There are three sizes of skewers: 6, 8, and 10 inches long. The longer ones are better for cooking on a barbecue grill. Skewers can often be a storage problem—getting mixed in with knives and other cooking utensils—so for convenience keep them in a tumbler near the stove.

Because beef is skewered more often than other types of food, the kind of meat you use is an important consideration. Since it is cooked very quickly under dry heat, it does not have the opportunity to tenderize. Therefore, it is essential that the meat be of the best quality, even if you are planning to marinate it beforehand. The loin and rib section, such as tenderloin (filet mignon), rib eye (Delmonico), and top sirloin are, by far, the choicest. Marinate tender chunks of meat for 3–5 hours; fish and poultry need no more than 1–2 hours of marination. Prick the pieces with a fork to help the marinade penetrate.

The pan that is used for skewering should be 1 inch deep and short enough so that the skewer handles protrude over the edge. Space the kebabs far apart on the skewer if you want them well done; close together for rare. The cooking time for perfect rare cubes of 1½ inches is 6 minutes, and keep skewers 3 inches or less from the fire for a charred surface.

When skewering chicken, it must first be boned, skinned, and cut into bite-size chunks. Use the breast meat in order to have the tenderest pieces and allow one breast per person. Braising is the better cooking method for chicken, to keep it moist, but if you want to broil, it will be necessary to baste often, cook it at a low temperature, and farther than 3 inches from the source of heat.

To skewer with fruits and vegetables, you must select slightly underripe produce and always undercook it rather than overcook. One minute too long and they will lose all their heat-soluble vitamins. Since some vegetables require longer cooking time, you could parboil them first. Or add the fast-cooking ones toward the end of cooking on the tips of the skewers.

STIR FRYING

Stir frying is one of the most efficient methods of preparing food. It is quick and it preserves the food's original freshness and vitality, provided the cook is organized and follows a few basic rules.

First, everything that you plan to stir fry must be washed, cut, and ready to go into the pan, preferably in the order of cooking time. Meat is always first because vegetable juices and cooking liquids (sherry, soy sauce) can toughen meat if it hasn't already been partially cooked. Vegetables require less heat and more cooking time. Everything should be cut into bite-size pieces so they will cook quickly and evenly.

Heat the wok next. If you do not have a wok, any large skillet that conducts heat well (aluminum is best) will do perfectly. If your stove is electric, you may want to heat two burners—one very hot and another at medium heat—so you can move the pan from one to the other quickly rather than turning the heat-control knobs up and down and waiting for the burners to adjust. In stir-fry cooking, speed is essential to keep food from overcooking and losing its fresh look and taste.

After the skillet is hot, add a small amount of vegetable oil (peanut is recommended). Next, season the oil with fresh chopped garlic, ginger, or capsicums, or any spice you like. A shortcut used in Chinese restaurants is to keep a mixture of peanut oil, garlic, and salt on hand with which to douse the pan whenever it gets dry.

When adding the meat, there are two things to watch for. First, the meat must be dry in order for it to be seared. If it has been marinating, pat it dry with a paper towel; otherwise it will steam cook in the pan. The object of searing is for the high heat to trap the juices inside of the meat. Secondly, add only a pound of meat at a time. Anything more would decrease the temperature of the pan. If you have more than one pound, divide it and cook in small batches. The meat should be only partially cooked at this point.

HOW TO WRAP *EN PAPILLOTE*

As soon as beef turns brown, chicken becomes white, or shrimp is pale pink, temporarily remove it, returning it to the pan after the vegetables are cooked. Pork is the only meat left in the pan throughout the entire cooking time, and that is to ensure its being thoroughly cooked.

To stir fry fish select a firm-textured type, such as sea bass, so it will not crumble in the pan. Fish in general does not hold up well in the stir-frying process, therefore it is necessary to give it a protective coating before tossing it into the searing pan. Steep pieces of fish in a mixture of egg white and cornstarch, then cook briefly in oil if you want the fish to have a firm, crunchy coating, in water for a soft one.

Vegetables should be added to the skillet a fistful at a time so that oil is kept at a high temperature. Root vegetables such as carrots should go in first. Vegetables that contain a lot of water (mushrooms, cabbage, and celery) follow. If you need to add more oil, do so in a wide circular motion inside the rim so that it is heated by the metal as it runs down the sides before it touches the vegetables or meat. The liquid seasonings should be added in the same manner as the oil.

WRAP COOKING

The "wraps" for wrap cooking are a stimulus for the imagination. People use cabbage leaves, corn husks, papaya leaves, grape leaves, and good old aluminum foil. The purpose behind it all is to seal in moisture and to impart interesting flavors and textures mainly to fish and meat.

To prepare lettuce leaves, briefly soak them in boiling water. Drain, dry, and fill. Wrap them in the leaf-packets (see illustration) and tie or place seam side down. In a casserole, melt 2 tablespoons butter and 2 cups boiling water or stock. Put food into the casserole and place a plate on top. Bake or simmer for 35–40 minutes if filling is uncooked, 10 minutes if it is precooked.

TIPS

FREEZING

Speed is the most important factor in freezing. Waste no time between washing, carving out any bad spots, wrapping or enclosing the food securely, and placing it in a freezer at 0 degrees or below. Higher temperatures cause changes in flavor, texture, and color. All packages, when first inserted into the freezer, should touch freezer walls but not each other for the greatest exposure to the chilling air. Food needs to freeze very quickly, so don't overload the freezer.

Always label and date what you freeze and use the oldest first. Remember when filling a container that food expands during freezing, so allow 1–1½ inches of space between the top and the food. Then put in a crumbled piece of wax paper to keep fruit or vegetables from poking up out of liquid and discoloring.

Do not season food that is going to be frozen. Pepper, garlic, and vanilla intensify in flavor and salt completely diminishes. Also, do not stuff a bird before freezing it. You run the risk of contaminating the meat. With poultry freeze the bird—whole or in pieces—just as you plan to serve it. A cut-up chicken takes up much less space than a whole one.

Meat and fish keep better when they are lean. Fish must be cleaned, eviscerated, cut the way you plan to eat it (fillets or steaks), and frozen the day it is bought or caught.

Casseroles and stews freeze well if there is plenty of sauce to cover the meat, fish, or fowl. Other foods that freeze well are stuffed pepper, Swiss steak, baked beans, hash, meat loaf, chicken fricassee, Valencia oranges, berries, peaches (allow peaches to sit at room temperature for 2–3 days), and cherries.

HOW TO WRAP FOR FREEZING

THE DRUGSTORE FOLD

THE BUTCHER WRAP

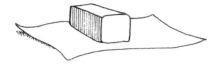

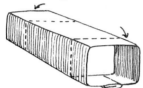

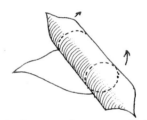

Roll folded edge down, turn over

Fold ends of roll down

Ends up and over, tuck tight

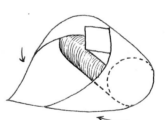

Sides over end

Tuck sides in

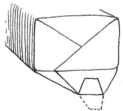

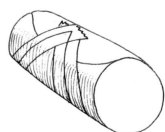

Fold tip of point over

Roll to end of paper— seal open edges with tape

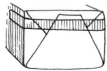

Fold up and tape

Butter and margarine can be frozen in store wrappers. (Unsalted keeps better than salted.) Cheese can be frozen in small packages to keep it from drying out. Milk can be frozen; nuts and coffee are better when stored in the freezer. They take 4 hours to thaw. Eggs can be frozen if they are first broken and lightly beaten. Do not freeze potatoes, pasta, mayonnaise, caviar, custard, cream pies, cream cheese, cottage cheese, or vegetables that contain a lot of water.

MARINATING

The purpose of marinating food is to flavor, tenderize, and preserve it. A marinade consists of a sharp, acidic liquid that breaks down the tough fibers in meat, oil that carries flavorings and lubricates, and seasonings. The acidic liquids can be wine, lemon or lime juice, vinegar, yogurt, or soy sauce.

The difference between marinades and barbecue sauces is that meat soaks in marinades *prior* to cooking. A large fish or cut of meat can be marinated for 5 days. Smaller fish or chopped meat is marinated overnight and ground meat for 1–2 hours. If you want a marinade to serve also as a barbecue sauce, add melted butter to it and the meat won't need basting. It will adhere to the meat chunks. Summer is a very good time to marinate because it preserves meat and fish in hot weather. Usually only seafood is refrigerated when marinating. Meat can stand at room temperature for not longer than 24 hours.

Marinades can also be used as cooking sauces too. Just thicken with a little cornstarch, arrowroot, flour, or egg yolk. One very important tip about marinating is not to use red wine for marinating chicken unless you want blue chicken!

PRESERVING COLOR

There are many different ways to preserve the color of food. Using ascorbic acid, citric acid, and lemon juice are probably the most common, with varying degrees of effectiveness. Others are blanching, commercial preparations, and vinegar.

For fruit, ascorbic acid is the best. The pure crystalline form, available at a drug store, is the most effective. Use 1 teaspoon, which is equal to 3,000 milligrams. You can also use vitamin C tablets in doses of 400–500 milligrams. Crush one between two spoons and dissolve in water or juice. Boil the liquid, then cool. It is best for apples, apricots, nectarines, peaches, and pears.

For meat, ascorbic acid is also the best buy. It not only keeps a good hold on color but it acts as a warning signal. When it begins to lose its effectiveness and the color starts to drain out of the meat, that means bacteria has reached an unhealthy level. Use ¼ teaspoon pure crystalline ascorbic acid for every 5 pounds of meat.

Vegetables that are to be frozen will preserve their color if they are blanched in boiling water. Blanch them in steam if they are to be dried. Vegetables such as string beans, broccoli, brussels sprouts, cauliflower, peas, spinach, and turnips will keep color if you blanch them before cooking. Drop them into a big pot of boiling water for 4 minutes, drain quickly, and cover with ice-cold water to stop the cooking process. After they've cooled, cook according to your recipe directions but allow a little less time.

Other methods for preserving the color of peas are, after boiling, submerge them in ice-cold water for a second. Or when cooking, add a few pods to the water.

A dash of vinegar after potatoes and cauliflower have boiled will whiten them. When cooking green vegetables to be eaten right away, add a little lemon juice to the cooking water. Lemon juice and citric acid preserve seafood for canning. Reconstituted lemon juice and a fresh lemon are equally effective, but be careful of using too much, for it will mask the food's flavor.

RIPENING

Sun-ripened fruits and vegetables are best. Flavorful and nutritious, they've come to full maturity before picking. Unfortunately, most produce comes to market before it is fully ripened. Therefore, choose produce that is closest in color and texture to what it is like when ripe.

Deep-red tomatoes; crisp, green lettuce; pears with a blush of red; pineapples with leaves that can be easily pulled out and which are turning slightly yellow; melons that yield when touched at the stem end, are all examples of ripe produce. Broccoli should not have yellow buds; peppers shouldn't pucker; bean sprouts and mushrooms should be bright white and firm. Beware of produce that has been sprayed with preservatives, such as packaged mushrooms. They don't show their age but you will taste it. Asparagus are more tender if they're thin. When buying artichokes, select those with tightly closed buds—not those starting to open.

Many people think that buying vegetables with their greens attached (e.g., carrots, radishes, and beets) ensures that they are getting fresher vegetables than those in plastic bags. Not necessarily. They *might* be fresher, but the green tops are sapping the nutrients out of the root vegetable, and the vegetable can no longer get replacements from the soil. It would be wise when eating carrots, radishes, and beets to eat the greens as well.

Buying an avocado at its perfect ripeness can be a matter of luck. If you have to buy a stone-hard one, ripen it at home by putting it in a wool sock and hiding it in a dark place. Put other unripened fruit in a paper bag and leave for a few days.

CANNING

Canning is a process of storing fruits and vegetables in airtight containers so that they are protected from spoilage or contamination. In order for you to enjoy the results of your canning, there are some important principles to follow along with a few specific tips. The following paragraphs are general instructions. You should be sure to consult another source for specific details.

First, it is essential that all utensils, equipment, surfaces, and food be kept very clean throughout the entire process. This in mind, always use new rubber rings and glass or metal lids. Jars can be reused. They must have either vacuum-seal metal covers, rubber rings with solid metal screw tops, a glass top with two bails, or a glass top and screwbands. Examine jars for nicks or cracks by running your finger along the edges. Rubber-ring jars should be tested for leakage by half filling them with hot water, sealing, and inverting them. Test the jar rubbers by folding them over and squeezing them. The rubber should not crack. Scrub jars carefully with hot sudsy water or sterilize in boiling water for 10 minutes. Keep rubbers in hot water until ready to use.

Select only the best quality produce for your canning. Fruits and tomatoes should be fully ripe, uniform in size, washed thoroughly of soil, with all blemishes removed. Vegetables will be more flavorful if they are picked slightly young and tender. Can within 2 hours of obtaining produce. All nonacid fruits and all vegetables (anything with a pH of 4.5 or higher) should be canned in a pressure canner to prevent botulism. Pressure canners come with complete operating instructions.

Fruit does not have to be canned in syrup. Sugar adds flavor and it will keep fruit firm, but fruit can be kept perfectly in its own juice or in boiling water. A syrup is good for canning fruits that are not highly acidic or that are naturally sour, such as rhubarb.

When filling the jars, set a wide funnel into the mouth and fill to half an inch from the top. Pack hot vegetables (corn, peas, and shellbeans especially) loosely. Tomatoes, however, need to be pressed down to squeeze out the excess juice. Raw food, in general, is packed firmly, over which hot juice or water (not boiling and not cold, because the jar will crack) is added.

To process filled jars, you'll need a large covered kettle. Only process one jar at a time—instead of assembly-line style—completely sealing it before starting the next so that contents of opened jars are not spoiled by the air. There must be enough water so it is over the jars by an inch, and there needs to be a rack on the bottom of the kettle so the jars won't touch the base. As you are filling the kettle with jars, make sure you set the jars half an inch apart from each other and gradually increase the heat so that there is a full rolling boil by the time the kettle is full. Begin timing the process at the beginning of the boil.

After jars are removed from the kettle, completely seal and set them on towels or newspapers out of a draft. Don't invert and *don't open* the jars. After 24 hours check the condition of the seals. If they are loose, if you see any bubbles or seepage, use the food immediately or reprocess it using a new lid. Wipe off any dried canning liquid. Label. Store in a cool dark place.

DRYING

Food that you want to dry must be in its freshest and ripest condition. Handle it quickly—peel it, slice it, pit it—good drying is done fast so the food won't decompose before it dries.

Just about any fruit is suitable for drying. Those which produce the best results are apples, bananas (do not use green, only those developing brown spots), figs, grapes (seedless), papayas, peaches, pears, and plums. Those that aren't quite as adaptable but still turn out fairly good are berries, cherries, coconut, dates, guavas, nectarines, pineapple (must be very ripe), rhubarb, and organic lemon and orange rind. It is a custom in Turkey to even dry whole lemons!

The best vegetables to use are cabbage, carrots, celery, corn, cucumber, mushrooms, onions, parsley, peas, peppers, potatoes, tomatoes, and zucchini.

If you have a garden, pick your fruit, vegetables, and herbs during the late morning on a dry sunny day. That way you can be assured that the crop will be carrying very little moisture on its outer skins or leaves. With herbs, pick the top leaves from the young plants. If you are picking food off of wild plants, be careful that you are far from a highway. Plants are veritable sponges of toxic fumes.

Herbs are relatively easy to dry. You can use either the summer or the winter method. With the summer method, after picking the herbs tie them by the stalks into large bunches and put each bunch into a paper bag. Hang the bags from the ceiling of a screened-in porch or any room that gets plenty of ventilation. They should dry in 24 hours. To dry herbs in the winter, remove the leaves from the stalks, put the leaves on a plate, and place them in a warm oven. When thoroughly dry, take them out and rub between your palms into a powder. Store in airtight bottles.

Drying whole foods can be done in an oven, out of doors, in a homemade dryer, or a commercial one.

The ideal temperature for drying food is 90–110 degrees Fahrenheit. Anything higher and the food loses its vitamins and flavor. If you're using an oven, set it on the lowest temperature (approximately 140 degrees) and put the tray no less than 8 inches above the heat source. If the oven has no air vents, as in some electric ovens, leave the door ajar. Do not overload the oven and be sure to stagger the trays so the drying air can zigzag its way up.

The trays should be shallow and wooden—never metal—approximately 12–16 inches wide, 16–20 inches long, and 1–2 inches deep. The crates that produce such as kiwi fruit come in, are perfect for this. Line the bottom with cheesecloth or an old sheet to keep sugary foods from sticking. Fruit that is dried whole can benefit from blanching, which will crack the skin, enabling moisture to escape freely. When drying halves of fruit, place the skin side down on the tray. The fruit won't stick and will dry faster.

A food that is very nearly dry will start to rattle on the tray. Test it by slicing with a knife. If no juice escapes and the fruit feels springy, leathery, and sticky or the vegetable feels brittle or tough, you have a finished product.

Outdoor drying is best accomplished in an ideal climate—that is, warm dry heat. If you live in the Southwest, the interior of California, or the western plains states, you can dry food to your heart's content. Those of us in the notoriously humid Northeast, South, and Northwest will have to wait for the perfect day. Do not even consider outdoor drying if you live in a large city, a smog belt, or near a major thruway.

SMOKING

There are two ways of smoking meat. One is called "hot smoking," which means cooking meat or fish in a smoky barbecue for several hours until it is ready to be eaten. This can be done inside your home. The other method of smoking involves a slow, smoldering smoke that ranges between 70–90 degrees Fahrenheit, and does not cook the meat. It is more of a treatment for meat prior to cooking.

Generally, the hot-smoke method uses a barbecue grill and a heavy skillet filled with wood chips. This process can take eight hours, and you must keep replacing wood chips all the while.

In order to do "cold smoking," you need to have the basic units of a smokehouse. These include an underground fire pit and a smoke chamber with a smoke tunnel running between the two. For the chamber, people use metal barrels, unused refrigerators, wooden boxes, etc.— anything that enables you to suspend the meat inside of it and from which you can cut a hole out of the top and bottom for the smoke to filter in and out.

Stovepipe is excellent to use for the tunnel, and the pit can be an old kettle. Both the pit and the tunnel must be underground about 2–2½ feet, and the pit animal-proofed with a metal lid.

The wood chips that produce the smoke are the fun and interesting aspect of smoking because they are like different spices and seasonings. Use chips from only hardwood trees— those that lose their leaves in the winter. Hickory is the most popular; apple and cherry are the sweetest; and maple, birch, chestnut, and ash all have wonderful smells and tastes. The reason for not using softwoods (pines, spruce, hemlock, balsam, and cedar) is that they give off a pitch that coats the meat and leaves a bad taste.

SALTING

Salting, or curing, is a means of flavoring and preserving food by impregnating it with a heavy dosage of salt. Curing is usually used for meat and often prior to smoking it, but vegetables can be salted as well. *Never use iodized or table salt, only pure medium-coarse pickling salt.*

There are two methods of curing: dry salting and brining. Dry salting is using simply salt to draw the water out of the food. Especially juicy or finely chopped vegetables can benefit from dry salting. Vegetables are brined only when they won't release enough of their own moisture to form the liquid for a proper cure.

Brining is salt added to ice-cold water or juice. It is used mostly for meats because salt by itself will dry meat out. Honey or maple syrup is also added to counteract the heavy taste of salt.

The things to consider when salting meat are that it is absolutely fresh to start with, that it's properly handled and chilled, that all of your equipment is sterile, and that the salt content is appropriate. A 15-percent solution (1½ cups salt to 5½ pints of juice/water) prevents the growth of salt tolerant bacteria.

Equipment for Salting:

large jars
wooden kegs or small barrels (new or thoroughly scrubbed)
safe cold storage area (36–38 degrees Fahrenheit)
moisture-proof wrapping for meat and fish plus a stocking for holding wrap tightly
plates or covers that fit down inside barrels or containers
weights for covers that will keep everything under brine

RECONSTITUTING

You can reconstitute dried fruit and vegetables to use them in a cooked dish, such as pies, casseroles, or cream desserts. Put them in a saucepan and just barely cover them with boiling water. Simmer for approximately 15 minutes, remove from heat, and let cool. If the fruit needs sweetening, do not add sugar until after cooking time, for it will toughen the fibers of the fruit.

The small amount of water from the reconstituting process has absorbed many nutrients and is comparable to fruit or vegetable juice, so add it to whatever you're making.

Another method is to put the fruit or vegetables into a bowl, pour boiling water just to the top of the dried food, cover the bowl, and let it soak up the water for several hours.

Homemade mayonnaise has a reputation for curdling, mainly because it has been stored at too cold a temperature. Move it to your refrigerator door shelf. To reconstitute mayonnaise that has transformed from a smooth, creamy sauce into a mass of oil and goop, there are several methods:

- Add 4 tablespoons of plain (unsalted) melted butter, which must be cold, into a round-bottom basin and gradually work in mayonnaise.
- Add 1 teaspoon prepared mustard to a hot dry bowl. Then add 1 tablespoon of the curdled mayonnaise. Beat with a wire whisk until smooth and thick. Continue to add 1 tablespoon of mayo at a time and beat well after each addition.
- Put one egg yolk in a bowl and gradually beat in mayonnaise.
- With an electric beater beat the mayonnaise briskly and add a splash of sweet cream and a pinch of sugar.

STORING

After grocery shopping you return home with a variety of tin cans, cardboard boxes, plastic bags, and glass jars. The best place to keep these items is in a dark, dry place that stays around 70 degrees. Hot moist environments cause food to develop mold and attract bugs. Even sunlight can destroy the vitamin content of food. Pantry shelves, a cupboard *not* above your stove, or a storage area in your basement are all ideal places to store things.

When buying starchy products (pasta, flour, bread crumbs, cereal, peas, and beans), choose the small-size packages so they will be used up quicker and transfer the contents to a glass jar with a screw-top lid. It's a good idea to do this with brown sugar also so it will stay soft.

Be sure to rotate the food so that the oldest is eaten first. Six months is the length of time that evaporated milk, nonfat dry milk, condensed soups, dried fruit stored in metal, and canned juices will keep. Twelve months is the limit for canned fish, hydrogenated fats and oils, flour, dry cereals stored in metal, uncooked cereal in its package, canned nuts, instant puddings, baking soda and powder, and bouillon. For canned meat, vegetables (except tomatoes and sauerkraut), and canned fruit, eighteen months is the limit.

HERBS AND SPICES

It is best to buy herbs and spices whole. Just before using them crumble the leaves between your palms or grind them in a peppermill, coffee grinder, or pestle and mortar. Fresh-grinding is your assurance that the spices will taste their best. When shopping for herbs and spices, test with your eyes and nose. The greener the herb or the redder the spice means the better the quality. Spices that are bought in glass containers may have been exposed to fluorescent lights for months. Store your dried herbs away from heat in a dry, dark place and in airtight containers. Dried herbs rarely have a shelf life of longer than four months. If you want to add dry herbs to a sauce, put them in boiling water for less than a minute, strain, and pat dry. They'll be greener and more flavorful.

Allspice: berry of the allspice tree; native to the West Indies. Used principally in marinades, curries, and pickling fruits and vegetables. Good in pot roast, meat loaf, baked ham, stewed chicken, Swedish meatballs.

Anise: licoricelike flavor. Use sparingly, whole or crushed, in cookies, candies, fruit pies, compotes, applesauce, and spicecake. Adds flavor to warm milk or tea.

Basil: delicate and fragrant. Best with tomatoes, in cold salads, with seafood and cucumbers. Crush leaves just before adding.

Bay: has a refreshing, woodsy flavor. Excellent in soups, sauces, and stews. Use ½ leaf of the dried, 1 whole leaf of the fresh. Good with shrimp, crab, salmon, and lobster.

Caraway seed: characteristic flavor in German and Scandinavian bread. Used as a digestive aid. Add whole to potatoes, cabbage, beets, seasoned butters.

Cardamom: dried seed prevalent in Scandinavian pastries. Apropos in curry powders. For a different taste, try a bruised seed in a cup of after-dinner coffee.

Cayenne: a powder ground from the seeds and pods of various peppers grown in the Cayenne district of Africa. Good in soups, sauces, eggs, and meats. Use sparingly.

Celery seed: from the flowers of the celery plant. It can be used in any dish calling for fresh celery. Best with cheese and cocktail juices, pastries, and sandwich spreads.

Chili powder: made with the ground pods of Mexican peppers plus cumin, garlic, and oregano. Adds flavor spark to corn, beans, rice, creamed seafood, and spareribs.

Chives: grow these in your garden or windowbox. Best when eaten fresh. Perfect in salads, egg dishes, and with cottage cheese.

Cinnamon: from the bark of the cinnamon tree. Use in sweet potatoes, squash, rice pudding, ham, cocoa, poultry stuffing. Whole sticks or ground.

Cloves: strong spicy-sweet flavor. Perks up chocolate, rice, and tapioca puddings. Best in gingerbread, applesauce, spicecake, beef stew.

Coriander: good in soups, stews, curry dishes, and chili. Seeds are also used to flavor frankfurters, homemade butterscotch candy, and exotic dishes from North Africa.

Cumin: fairly well known in Mexican and eastern Indian cuisine. Rub the seeds briskly between palms and let them fall into stews.

Curry powder: generally a blend of 10 or more spices, including turmeric, cardamom, coriander, mustard, saffron, and allspice. Good with chicken, eggs, seafood salads.

Dill: the leaves, chopped, go well with poached salmon, sour cream and cucumbers, eggs, cheeses, and steak. Seeds are an ingredient for pickles, sauerkraut, and apple pie. Sprigs can be used as a garnish.

Fennel: all of the plant—seeds, bulb, stalk, and leaves—is edible. Tastes licoricelike. Use the same as anise or serve cold and eat raw like celery.

Garlic: one of the oldest cultivated plants. A whole bulb will enrich a stew or sauce, or the juice from a clove can flavor a salad dressing. Garlic butter enhances steaks, chops, bread, and spaghetti.

Ginger: pungent and zesty. It gives life to oriental dishes, meat, chicken, glazed carrots, fruit salad dressings, pie crusts.

Juniper berries: a bluish-purple dried fruit with a bittersweet taste. Good in marinades, sauerkraut, and game.

Leeks: popular in French cuisine. It is best in soups or stews, or cooked and served with lemon butter or vinaigrette sauce.

Mace: the outer coating of the nutmeg seed. Similar to nutmeg in taste and uses. It complements chocolate, cherry dishes, cakes, cookies, preserves.

Marjoram: part of the mint family. Spicy. Good substitute for sage. Best in food that requires lengthy cooking.

Mint: usually used fresh. When adding to cooked foods, put mint in shortly before food finishes cooking. Complements peas and carrots, salads, yogurt.

Mustard: the seeds are used for pickling and salad dressings. The powder is delicious in tuna, ham, seafood, egg, and potato salads, vegetable relish, lobster bisque. Can be made into a paste by adding water, milk, white wine, or beer and letting it stand for 15 minutes.

Nutmeg: freshly grated is much better than commercially ground. Use in eggnog, chocolate, coffee cake, puddings, sweet potatoes.

Oregano: indispensable in Italian, Mexican, and Spanish cooking. It is also known as wild marjoram. Good in any tomato sauce dish, with sharp cheeses, in guacamole.

Paprika: pleasantly mild to exceptionally hot. Ground powder of a pepper plant. The best quality is a vibrant red. Sprinkle on cottage cheese, sour cream, baked fish, cole slaw.

Parsley: fresh is best, either curly or flat leaf. Can be used as a garnish. Brings out the flavor in food and other herbs.

Pepper: for the liveliest taste, buy whole black peppercorns and grind them in a mill. White pepper has the dark outer coating removed. It isn't quite as strong and is used in white sauces. Red pepper flakes, used sparingly, add color and spark to pasta and eggs.

Pepper pods: not related to peppercorns. Ripe when they are red. Use in Indian and Mexican cuisine.

Poppy seed: these tiny seeds, not from the same plant that produces opium, taste similar to walnuts and are best in desserts, breads, pastries, and buttered noodles.

Rocket: otherwise known as arugula in Italian markets or roquette by the French. Use it as a salad green. Sharp, peppery.

Rosemary: spicy; comparable to mint. Use in dumplings and biscuits, lamb, pork, poultry, and oranges.

Saffron: from the stamen of the autumn crocus. Adds flavor to rice, Spanish, and Italian dishes. Buy it in threads for a fresher flavor and steep it in hot liquid before using.

Sage: slightly bitter. Use with a light touch and don't cook long. Best in stuffings for fish or fowl.

Savory: it is best with peas, beans, and lentils, chilled vegetable juices, and meat loaf. Both winter and summer varieties have a wonderful aroma, but the "winter" has a stronger taste.

Sesame seed: toasted nut flavor, intensifies when seeds are baked or roasted. Blend with butter to make a spread. Add to green salads and French dressing.

Shallots: member of the onion family. Similar to garlic and scallions. Exceptional in salad dressings, sprinkled on steaks.

Sorrel: sour-leaf version of spinach. Best with fish (fatty types), green salads, potato soup.

Tarragon: Indispensable. Can be used with poultry, fish, meat, salads, veal, and eggs.

Thyme: use sparingly as background flavor. Pungent. Combines well with bay leaf for soups and stuffings.

Turmeric: related to ginger. Use in curry dishes, pickle relishes. Substitute for saffron.

HELPFUL HINTS

When steaming potatoes, cover them with a cloth then put the lid on the pan. They will cook faster and have a firmer texture.

To make lettuce or salad greens crisp, add 1 tablespoon of vinegar to a pan of water and let them soak for 15 minutes.

A dash of salt added to coffee that has boiled or been reheated too often will freshen the taste.

Black walnuts ground in a blender will enhance the flavor of pumpkin pie.

Mayonnaise separates when it gets too cold. Keep it in the door shelf of the refrigerator.

When measuring syrup or molasses, rinse the spoon or cup in cold water first and the liquid won't adhere to the utensil.

Mustard added to a salad dressing will hold the oil and vinegar together.

To clean a cheese grater easily, rub it with raw potato after using it.

To prevent fruit juice from running over in pies, sprinkle a little baking soda over the fruit before laying on the top crust.

A teaspoon of wine added to waffle batter will keep it from sticking to the waffle iron.

To cool a hot dish in a hurry, place it in a pan of *salted* water.

The greener leaves on the outside of a head of lettuce contain more vitamins than the inside leaves, so try not to discard them.

If the outside of bread or cake gets too brown before the inside is cooked, place a pan of warm water on the oven rack above it.

A pinch of salt added to flour before it is mixed with the liquid will keep gravy from getting lumpy.

Potatoes will bake faster if they are soaked in hot water for 15 minutes or in salt water for 20 minutes.

To keep egg yolks, cover with cold water and keep in the refrigerator.

When doubling a recipe, don't automatically double the spices until sampling.

Iced tea and coffee are improved if the ice cubes are made of tea and coffee.

Pastry will be flakier if a few drops of vinegar are added to the iced water.

Clams will open easier if boiling water is poured over them.

Lemons and limes won't turn brown if they are stored in water in the refrigerator.

A sprinkling of flour or cornstarch on top of a cake will prevent the frosting from running off.

Salt toughens eggs, so add it to egg dishes only after they are cooked.

If citrus fruits are warmed in the oven for a few minutes, they will be juicier.

Dried fruit and nuts will sink to the bottom of a cake unless rolled in cake flour first.

Spinach will clean faster in warm water.

When cooking cabbage, cauliflower, broccoli, or brussels sprouts, put a slice of white bread into the saucepan and it will absorb the odor. Spoon it out before removing the vegetables.

To tenderize tough vegetables, simmer them in milk rather than water. Expect the milk to curdle slightly.

A dash of nutmeg in any white sauce is a spectacular addition.

When a custard pie shrinks away from the crust it has been baked in too hot an oven.

Fresh bread will retain its shape if sliced with a hot knife.

If an egg cracks while it is boiling, lower the heat and pour a lot of salt on the crack. This will seal the egg, keeping the white from leaking into the water.

Eggs that have been accidentally cracked in the carton can be boiled wrapped in greased paper, such as a butter wrapper, or in aluminum foil twisted closed at both ends.

Bake apples, stuffed green peppers, and tomatoes in a well-greased muffin tin and they will retain their shape better.

Add 1 teaspoon baking powder to potatoes that are to be mashed and then beat vigorously. They will be extra light and creamy.

For an easy-to-make fruit salad dressing, combine 1 teaspoon grated orange rind, ⅓ cup orange juice, and 1 cup sour cream.

To freshen Italian or French bread, sprinkle crust with cold water and place it in oven preheated to 350 degrees Fahrenheit for 10 minutes.

Mustard added to a dish at the beginning of its cooking time will be less pungent than if it is added at the end.

Bury a length of vanilla bean in an airtight jar of sugar and keep the vanilla sugar on hand for baking.

To get rid of bad kitchen odors, boil several cloves in 1 cup of water.

Chewing gum while peeling onions will prevent tears.

A pinch of salt added to whipped cream will make it whip faster.

To keep milk from sticking to a pan, rub the bottom of the pan with butter.

The leftover rinds of oranges, lemons, and grapefruit can be grated and stored in an airtight jar in the refrigerator to use in cakes and frostings.

To keep a cake from falling when it is taken out of the oven, fill the pan with batter, lift it up, and drop it suddenly on a table. This will release the air bubbles.

When making meringue shells, line the baking sheet with brown paper (from a bag) cut to fit.

To plump up dried-out raisins, wash and put them in a shallow dish, then bake, covered, at 350 degrees Fahrenheit until puffy.

To make a fine-textured cake, add a few drops of boiling water to the butter and sugar when creaming.

PART II

How-To Information

MEASURING

To make the best possible recipe, you have to measure the ingredients accurately. Each measurement is designed to give you a particular result, just as each ingredient works together to form the delicious whole. Variations in these will change the outcome of the dish. The best way to know that you have measured correctly is to have the right measuring equipment.

MEASURING CUPS

Two sets of cups—one for dry measuring and one for liquid measuring—are necessary. Dry measure cups come in a set of four that includes ¼ cup, ⅓ cup, ½ cup, and 1 cup. They can be either metal or plastic.

For liquid measure, glass or clear plastic cups with a pouring spout come in 1-, 2-, and 4-cup sizes. They should have a little extra room at the top so liquids won't spill over.

MEASURING SPOONS

Standard sizes are ¼ teaspoon, ½ teaspoon, 1 teaspoon, and 1 tablespoon. They are used for both dry and liquid ingredients and shaped so they can be easily leveled off with a knife.

HOW TO MEASURE

Dry ingredients: loosely spoon ingredients into a measuring cup. Pile the cup high; don't shake or pack the contents down. Level off with a knife or metal spatula.

Liquid ingredients: set cup on a flat surface. Pour in liquid until it reaches the mark of the desired level.

Butter or margarine: sticks measure 8 tablespoons along their sides. Cut off what you need. Tub butter or margarine can be spooned out into a dry measuring cup and leveled off with a knife.

Solid shortening: with a rubber spatula, tightly fill a dry measuring cup, running the spatula through it to release air. Repack and level it off.

Brown sugar: the exception to measuring dry ingredients, brown sugar should be packed with your fingers down into the cup until it is level with the rim.

Shredded cheese: lightly fill dry measuring cup to rim. Do not pack.

SELECTING COOKING EQUIPMENT

POTS, SKILLETS, AND PANS

Always use good quality cookware. It will last longer and cook food better than poorly made equipment, which can burn easily—scorching your food, distribute heat unevenly, dent, and break. A strong pan with a sturdy, insulated handle and thick bottom is indispensable. It should also have a tight-fitting lid with a knob and sides that curve gently under at the bottom so there are no inaccessible areas for cooking utensils. Some useful, basic sizes are 1-2 cups, 1 quart, 2 quarts, and 8 quarts.

Skillets, or frying pans, are also essential. You'll need a 7-inch and a 12-inch. They should have covers, or you can get a flat lid, which works for many sizes. Nonstick surfaces are great for skillets, especially for crepes and omelets.

Aluminum cookware is a good, even conductor of heat, which is important for browning and sautéing. It is also lightweight and inexpensive. The one drawback is that it reacts chemically with acidic food.

Cast iron is the best for browning crusts. It evenly distributes and retains heat, and is the heaviest, most durable metal in cooking.

Copper pans are excellent heat conductors and are best used with food that requires exact timing and temperature. It is expensive, however, and it reacts chemically with all foods so the pans must always be lined with tin, which needs occasional replacing.

Stainless steel is lightweight and durable and doesn't react with foods. It is best used for cooking liquids. The material remains bright and tarnish-free, and is only moderately expensive. It does not conduct heat evenly so food might scorch if it is placed over a very hot burner.

Glass, porcelain, and earthenware all conduct heat well and can be transported from oven to table to refrigerator. Use for baking breads, pies, cakes, and casseroles.

KNIVES

The sharpness of a knife's cutting edge and the type of steel it is made of indicates its quality. Knives with a high carbon content have a harder blade and a sharper edge. They stay very sharp, but if they are not carefully dried after each washing, they will rust. Scouring them with steel wool will keep them rust-free and razor-edged.

Stainless steel knives will not rust and are easy to keep shiny. They do not hold their edge, however, so you need to resharpen them continually—and they are difficult to sharpen.

To test a knife for quality, hold the handle and see if you feel the center of gravity where the handle joins the blade. Check that the blade runs through the length of the handle (three rivets in the handle will indicate this), and that it tapers from the heel to the point and from the top of the blade to the cutting edge.

You will need one or two paring knives for peeling, seeding, and pitting; a utility knife for slicing fruit; a boning knife for boning chicken, fish, and beef; a slicing knife to thinly slice large chunks of meat; a butcher knife for cutting up raw meat and poultry; a French knife for chopping and mincing vegetables; and a serrated knife for cutting bread.

Do not keep knives loose in the drawer unless they are protected by sheaths. It is better to keep them in a slotted block of wood or on a magnetic rack.

FOR BAKING

Use shiny aluminum, stainless steel, or tin pans with smooth seams for easy cleaning when baking cakes, cookies, and muffins. These materials distribute heat evenly and give baked goods a golden brown crust. Always use the size of the pan that's specified in the recipe.

Cake pans: a pair of 8-inch and a pair of 9-inch circular pans, both 1½ inches deep, are good if you do a lot of baking. Also get an 8- or 9-inch square cake pan and a 9-inch by 12-inch rectangular pan. A 10-inch tube pan and bundt pan are also useful.

Pie pans: standard sizes are 8 and 9 inches. Purchase both. Recipes call for one as much as the other.

Loaf pans: come in two standard sizes, 9 by 5 by 3 and 8½ by 4½ by 2½. Either is good for breads, quick breads, and loaf cakes.

Muffin tins: come in many sizes but most recipes call for cups that hold ½ cup of batter.

Cookie sheets: buy at least two because you'll have a lot of cookie batter that should be cooked in batches.

Tart pans: 10-inch size with removable ring for tarts and quiches.

Jelly-roll pan: classic size is 10½ by 15½ by 1 inch. Small edge around the side keeps food from sliding off.

Soufflé dish: the 1-quart size is fine for individuals or small families; otherwise purchase the 2-quart. Dish should have upright sides and be made out of porcelain or glass.

Custard cups: glass or earthenware. Use for custard, miniature soufflés, and popovers.

Rolling pin: a large, heavy one is crucial for rolling out dough successfully.

Cake rack: air space between racks is necessary for cooling cakes, breads, and cookies.

Pastry blender: the wire strands evenly cut shortening or butter into flour.

OTHER USEFUL EQUIPMENT

_____ Bulb baster
_____ Chopping board
_____ Colander
_____ Electric mixer
_____ Funnel
_____ Grater
_____ Kitchen scissors
_____ Knife sharpener
_____ Mallet
_____ Metal utensils (spatula, pancake turner, slotted spoon, two-tined fork, ladle, potato masher)
_____ Mixing bowls
_____ Nutcracker

_____ Openers (bottle, can, corkscrew)
_____ Pepper grinder
_____ Rotary beater
_____ Rubber spatula
_____ Sifter
_____ Strainer
_____ Thermometers (meat, oven)
_____ Timer
_____ Tongs
_____ Vegetable parer
_____ Vegetable steamer
_____ Whisk
_____ Wooden spoons

PART III
Charts and Tables

CALORIES

Almonds, 10 nuts	60
Anchovies, canned, 5 fillets	35
Apple juice, bottled, 1 cup	117
Apples, fresh with skin, 1 average	61
Applesauce, canned, ½ cup	116
Apricots	
fresh, 3 average	55
canned, heavy syrup, ½ cup	111
dried, ½ cup	169
Asparagus	
boiled, 4 spears	12
canned, ½ cup	25
frozen, 6 spears	23
Avocados	
California	185
Florida	196
Bacon, fried, 3 slices	86
Bagel, 1 medium	165
Bananas, 1 small	81
Bean curd, 1 cake	86
Bean sprouts, soy, raw, ½ cup	24
Beans, baked with pork, tomato sauce, ½ cup	156
Beans, green, boiled, ½ cup	16
Beans, lima	
boiled, ½ cup	95
canned, ½ cup	82
frozen, ½ cup	106
Beans, red kidney, canned, ½ cup	115
Beef, choice grade cuts	
brisket, lean only, braised, 4 oz	253
chuck, lean only, broiled, 4 oz	282
club steak, lean only, broiled, 4 oz	277
flank steak, lean, simmered, 4 oz	222
ground, lean, broiled, 4 oz	248
porterhouse, lean, broiled, 4 oz	254
rib, lean, roasted, 4 oz	273
round steak, lean, broiled, 4 oz	214
rump, lean, roasted, 4 oz	253
sirloin, lean, broiled, 4 oz	245
T-bone, lean, broiled, 4 oz	253
Beet greens, boiled, drained, ½ cup	13
Beets, boiled, sliced, ½ cup	33

Blueberries	
fresh, ½ cup	45
canned, syrup, ½ cup	126
frozen, sweetened, ½ cup	121
Bologna, all meat, 4 oz	315
Bouillon cube, 1	5
Brazil nuts, 3 large	90
Bread, 1 slice	
cracked wheat	60
French	44
Italian	28
pumpernickel	79
raisin	60
rye, whole wheat	56
white	63
Broccoli, boiled, ½ cup	20
Brussels sprouts, boiled, ½ cup	28
Butter, 1 tbsp	100
Cabbage	
red, raw, shredded, ½ cup	14
white, raw, shredded, ½ cup	11
white, boiled, ½ cup	16
Cantaloupe, ½ melon	58
Carrots	
raw, 1 average	21
boiled, ½ cup	23
Cashew nuts, roasted, salted, 4 oz	639
Catsup, 1 tbsp	16
Cauliflower	
raw, ½ cup	12
boiled, ½ cup	14
Caviar, sturgeon, granular, 1 oz	74
Celery, raw, 1 stalk	7
Cheese, 1 oz	
American processed, Edam	105
Camembert, mozzarella	85
cheddar	113
cottage, large curd, ½ cup	120
cottage, small curd, ½ cup	112
cream	106
fontina	114
Gouda	108
Gruyère	110
monterey Jack	103

Muenster	100
parmesan	111
parmesan, grated, 1 tbsp	23
provolone	99
ricotta	45
romano	110
romano, grated, 1 tbsp	30
Roquefort	105
Swiss	104
Chestnuts, 10	141
Chicken	
broiled, meat, no skin, 4 oz	154
roasted, meat and skin, 4 oz	283
stewed, meat only, ½ cup	135
Chili, canned, ½ cup	170
Chives, 1 tbsp	1
Chocolate, bitter or baking, unsweetened 1 oz	143
Clams, raw, 4 oz	92
Coconut, dried, unsweetened, shredded, 4 oz	751
Cod, broiled with butter, fillets, 4 oz	192
Cookies	
brownies, iced with nuts	103
chocolate chip	50
cream sandwich	49
fig bar	50
gingersnaps	29
graham cracker	55
macaroon	91
molasses	137
oatmeal and raisin	59
peanut sandwich	58
shortbread	37
vanilla wafer	19
Corn	
boiled on cob	70
boiled, kernels, ½ cup	69
canned, cream style, ½ cup	105
Cornmeal, ½ cup	217
Cornstarch, 1 tbsp	29
Crab, canned, 4 oz	115
Crackers	
cheese, 1 oz	136
Melba toast, 1	15
oyster, 1 oz	112
Ritz, 1	16
Rye-Krisp, 1; Triscuits, 1	21
Saltines, 1	12

Cranberry juice, bottled, 1 cup	164
Cranberry sauce, canned, ½ cup	202
Cream	
Half-and-Half, ½ cup	162
sour, ½ cup	243
whipping, ½ cup	419
Cucumber, 6 slices	4
Dates, 10	219
Duck, roasted, meat only, 4 oz	352
Eclair	239
Eggplant, boiled, diced, ½ cup	92
Eggs	
raw, whole	82
raw, white	17
raw, yolk	59
boiled, poached	82
fried	99
scrambled	111
Fat, vegetable, shortening, 1 tbsp	111
Figs	
fresh, 1 small	32
dried, 1 large	57
Finnan haddie, 4 oz	117
Flounder fillets, baked, 4 oz	229
Flour	
all-purpose, sifted, 1 cup	419
cake, sifted, 1 cup	349
wheat, sifted, 1 cup	405
Frankfurters, all-meat, 1	133
Ginger root, fresh, 1 oz	14
Goose, roasted, meat and skin, 4 oz	503
Grape juice	
bottled, 1 cup	167
frozen, 1 cup	133
Grapes	
Concord, 10	18
Thompson, 10	34
Grapefruit	
pink, ½ average	58
white, ½ average	54
Grapefruit juice, frozen, 1 cup	101
Ham, roasted, 4 oz	426
Herring, pickled, 4 oz	253
Honey, 1 tbsp	64
Honeydew melon, diced, ½ cup	28

Horseradish, prepared, 1 tbsp	6
Ice cream, rich, 16% fat, ½ cup	165
Ice cream bar, chocolate covered, 3 oz	162
Jams and preserves, 1 tbsp	54
Jellies, 1 tbsp	49
Kale, boiled, ½ cup	22
Lamb chop, broiled, 4 oz	341
Lard, 1 tbsp	117
Leeks, raw, 3 average	52
Lemon juice	
fresh, 1 tbsp	4
bottled, 1 cup	56
Lemonade, frozen, diluted, 1 cup	107
Lemons, 1 average	20
Lentils, cooked, 1 cup	212
Lettuce	
Boston, 1 head	23
Iceberg, 1 head	70
Romaine, 3 leaves	5
Liver	
beef, fried, 4 oz	260
calf, fried, 4 oz	296
chicken, simmered, 4 oz	187
Liverwurst, 4 oz	362
Lobster, cooked, meat only, 4 oz	108
Macaroni, boiled, ½ cup	96
Mangoes, 1	152
Marmalade, 1 tbsp	51
Milk	
whole, 1 cup	159
buttermilk, 1 cup; skim, 1 cup	88
sweetened, condensed, 1 cup	982
evaporated, 1 cup	345
Muffin	
corn	130
English	140
Mussels, raw, 4 oz	130
Mustard, prepared, 1 tbsp	4
Nectarines, 1	88
Noodles, egg, cooked, ½ cup	100
Oil	
corn, safflower, sesame, 1 tbsp	120
olive, peanut, 1 tbsp	119
Okra, boiled, 10 pods	41
Olives, green, 10 large	45

Orange juice	
fresh, 1 cup	120
frozen, diluted, 1 cup	112
Oranges, 1	63
Oysters	
east coast, 2–3	19
west coast, 6–9	218
Pancakes, plain, buttermilk, 4 in	61
Papaya, 1	119
Parsley, 1 tbsp	2
Parsnips, boiled, mashed, ½ cup	70
Pâté de foie gras, 1 oz	131
Peaches	
fresh, 1	38
canned, syrup, ½ cup	100
dried, ½ cup	210
Peanut butter, commercial, 1 tbsp	94
Peanuts	
raw, shelled, 4 oz	640
roasted, halves, ½ cup	421
Pears	
Bartlett	100
Bosc	86
D'Anjou	122
canned in syrup, 4 oz	87
dried, ½ cup	241
Peas, boiled, ½ cup	57
Pecans, 10	62
Peppers, green, raw, ½ cup	17
Peppers, red, raw, chopped, ½ cup	24
Pickle relish, 1 tbsp	17
Pickles	
dill, 1	15
sour, 1	14
sweet, 1	22
Pineapple	
fresh, diced, ½ cup	41
canned in syrup, 4 oz	84
Pineapple juice, canned, 1 cup	138
Pistachio nuts, shelled, ½ cup	372
Plums, 1	66
Pomegranates, 1	97
Popcorn	
popped plain, 1 cup	23
oil and salt, 1 cup	41
Pork chop, broiled, 4 oz	308

Potato chips, 10	114
Potatoes	
baked in skin	145
boiled, peeled	88
french fried	137
mashed with milk, butter, ½ cup	99
Potatoes, sweet	
baked in skin	161
candied, 1	176
Pretzels, 1 oz	111
Prune juice, bottled, 1 cup	197
Prunes, dried, 1	16
Pumpkin, canned, ½ cup	41
Radishes, raw, 10	14
Raisins, 4 oz	328
Raspberries	
black, fresh, ½ cup	49
red, fresh, ½ cup	35
Rhubarb, cooked, sweetened, ½ cup	191
Rice, cooked, long-grain	
brown, ½ cup	116
white, ½ cup	112
Rolls	
dinner	83
hamburger/frankfurter	119
Kaiser	156
raisin	78
sweet	89
Salad dressings, 1 tbsp	
blue cheese	76
French	66
Italian	83
mayonnaise	101
Thousand Island	80
Salami, 1 slice	68
Salmon	
steak, broiled, 4 oz	207
canned, pink, 4 oz	160
smoked, 4 oz	200
Sauces	
soy, 1 tbsp	74
Worcestershire, 1 tbsp	15
Sausage, pork	
1 link	62
Shrimp, fresh, breaded, fried, 4 oz	255
Soda, 1 cup	
club	0
cola	96

cream	105
ginger ale	76
root beer	100
7-Up	97
tonic	76
Spaghetti	
boiled, ½ cup	96
Spinach, boiled, ½ cup	21
Squash, summer	
yellow, boiled, ½ cup	14
zucchini, boiled, ½ cup	14
Squash	
acorn, baked, ½ squash	86
butternut, baked, ½ cup	70
Strawberries	
fresh, ½ cup	28
frozen, sliced, sweetened, ½ cup	139
Sugar	
brown, ½ cup	411
brown, 1 tbsp	52
granulated, ½ cup	385
granulated, 1 tbsp	46
powdered, ½ cup	231
powdered, 1 tbsp	31
maple, 4 oz	395
Swordfish, broiled, 4 oz	186
Syrup	
corn, 1 tbsp	58
molasses, 1 tbsp	43
Tangerine, 1	39
Tomato juice	
bottled, 1 cup	46
paste, ½ cup	108
Tomatoes, raw, 1 average	20
Tuna, in oil, drained, ½ cup	158
Turkey	
dark meat, roasted, 4 oz	230
light meat, roasted, 4 oz	200
Veal, loin, broiled, 4 oz	245
Vinegar, cider, 1 tbsp	2
Walnuts, English, 10	322
Water chestnuts, raw, whole, 5–7	79
Watercress, raw, ½ cup	4
Watermelon, 1 average wedge	111
Wheat germ, 1 tbsp	23
Yeast, brewer's dry, 1 oz	80
Yogurt, plain, whole milk	152

GLOSSARY

al dente: an Italian phrase that means "to the tooth" and refers to cooking pasta tender but firm.

amandine: made or served with almonds.

arrowroot: an American tropical plant whose root yields a nutritive starch that can be used as a thickening agent.

aspic: a jelly made from stock or tomato juice and gelatin.

bard: to tie a thin layer of fat around lean meats to keep them from drying out in cooking.

beard: to cut the hairy fibers off unshucked mussels.

béarnaise: a rich egg sauce flavored with wine and herbs.

béchamel: a basic white sauce.

bisque: a creamy soup with a shellfish base.

blanc, au: poached or simmered and served in a white sauce.

bordelaise: a basic brown sauce with bordeaux wine for part of the liquid.

bouillabaisse: a stew of different kinds of fish and shellfish.

bouquet garni: a small bunch of dried or fresh herbs tied in cheesecloth and used to flavor stocks and stews; it consists of parsley, thyme, tarragon, bay leaf, marjoram, and chervil.

bourguignonne: a rich sauce of burgundy wine, braised onions, and mushrooms.

braise: to brown in fat then cook, covered, on the stove top or in the oven with a small amount of liquid and seasoning.

brine: to preserve in a strong salt solution, or the solution itself.

bruise: to crush partially in a pestle and mortar to release flavor, as with cardamom, garlic cloves, or peppercorns.

butterfly: to split food down the center not quite all the way so the two halves open like butterfly wings.

caramelize: to melt granulated sugar in a heavy saucepan over very low heat until sugar is liquid and brown.

chapon: a cube or chunk of bread rubbed with oil and garlic and tossed with salad to impart a subtle flavor. Discard before serving. An alternative method: rub the salad bowl with the chapon before greens are added.

chateaubriand: a thick fillet of beef.

clarify: to make a cloudy liquid clear.

coat a spoon: a doneness test for sauces, custards, and soups. A spoon dipped into a cream soup should have a thin film when withdrawn. Dipped into a sauce made for covering food, it should emerge with a thick coating.

coddle: to poach in water just below the boiling point.

compote: fruits stewed in a light syrup.

coquille: a scallop or shell, or a dish served in shells.

court bouillon: liquid in which fish is cooked, containing water, white wine, vegetables, herbs, salt, and pepper.

crimp: to seal the edge of a pie or pastry with an attractive edge.

cut and fold: to cut through a mixture with a spoon or spatula, turn, and mix from the bottom.

cut in shortening: to mix shortening into dry ingredients with fingers, two knives, or pastry blender, until it is mealy.

deglaze: after meat, fish, or poultry has been roasted or sautéed, and the pan degreased, liquid is poured into the pan and all flavorful cooking juices are scraped up and simmered. It can be used as a sauce by itself or in addition to others.

dredge: to coat with seasoned flour, bread or cracker crumbs, or sugar.

drizzle: to sprinkle drops of butter, syrup, or sauce over the surface of food in a fine stream.

duchesse: potatoes mashed with cream, enriched with egg yolk, and pressed out through a pastry tube.

dust: to coat lightly with flour, confectioner's sugar, or any powder mixture. More lightly coated than dredged.

flan: open custard or fruit tart.

florentine: food served with or on a bed of spinach, often creamed.

fluff: to fork up until light and fluffy.

flute: to make a decorative edge on pies, pastries, or to cut mushrooms or other small vegetables into scalloped shapes.

fricassee: a stew of chicken, rabbit, or veal in white sauce.

frizzle: to fry thinly sliced meat at intense heat until crisp and curled.

glaze: to cover food with glossy coating, syrup, vinegar, aspic, jellies.

gratiné: to brown the top of a sauced dish under the broiler. Bread crumbs, grated cheese, and butter help form crust.

leaven: to lighten the texture and increase the volume of breads, cakes, cookies by using baking soda, powder, or yeast.

meunière, à la: sautéed food, most often fish, served with butter and lemon sauce.

mince: to chop very fine. After chopping roughly with one hand on top of the blade and the other on the handle, rock blade back and forth from one end of pile to the other to chop into desired sized bits.

mornay: a rich sauce with melted cheese.

nap: to cover food with a cream sauce which is thick enough so that it doesn't hide outline of food.

parboil: to cook briefly in boiling water or seasoned liquid or in a skillet over direct heat with little fat.

pâte: a paste, dough, or frying batter.

pâté: a pie or spread containing ground meat, fish, or poultry and served cold.

pilaf: a dish flavored with saffron, turmeric and meat, poultry, or fish.

praline: flavored with browned almonds and browned in syrup.

purée: to grind a paste, to mash to a smooth blend.

ragout: a rich, brown stew with meat and vegetables.

refresh: plunge hot food into ice-cold water in order to cool it immediately, stop the cooking process, and preserve color.

render: to heat lard or other animal fat so that it melts away from connective tissue and turns into a pure, smooth, and creamy substance. Use double boiler, press down on fat with spoon with cooking. Perfect for pastry.

scallop: the verb means to bake with a sauce or cream.

score: to make shallow cuts in long lines in the meat and fish to keep them from curling up when broiled.

shirr: to cook whole eggs in a small baking dish with cream and often a topping of bread crumbs, buttered.

sorbet: a partially frozen ice made of water, fruit, and liqueur.

spin a thread: to cook a syrup to 238 degrees, at which point a thin brittle thread forms when a spoon is taken out of the boiling liquid.

stiff but not dry: describes beaten egg whites that stand up in stiff, moist peaks.

stock: the broth strained from stewed or boiled meats, seafood, poultry, or vegetables.

stud: to insert whole cloves or slivers of garlic into the surface of food.

swirl: to whirl liquid gently in a pan.

truss: to bind a bird into a compact shape before roasting.

SUBSTITUTIONS

allspice, 1 teaspoon = ½ teaspoon cinnamon plus ⅛ teaspoon ground cloves

baking powder, 1 teaspoon = 1 teaspoon baking soda plus 1 teaspoon cream of tartar, or ¼ teaspoon baking soda plus ½ cup buttermilk or sour milk (to replace ½ cup of liquid)

cake flour, 1 cup = 1 cup all-purpose flour minus 2 tablespoons

chicken broth, 1 cup canned = 1 cube or 1 envelope plus 2 cups boiling water

chocolate, 1 square unsweetened = 3 tablespoons cocoa plus 1 tablespoon butter or margarine

cornstarch, 1 tablespoon = 2 tablespoons flour or 4 teaspoons quick-cooking tapioca

corn syrup, 1½ cups = 1 cup sugar plus ½ cup water

egg, 1 whole = 2 egg yolks plus 1 tablespoon water

flour, 1 cup presifted = 1 cup plus 2 tablespoons cake flour

garlic, 1 clove = ⅛ teaspoon garlic powder

ginger, 1 tablespoon raw = ⅛ teaspoon ginger powder

herbs, 1 tablespoon fresh = 1 teaspoon dried

honey, ⅔ cup = 1 cup sugar plus ⅓ cup water

Italian seasoning, 1 teaspoon = ¼ teaspoon each of oregano, basil, thyme, rosemary plus dash of cayenne

lemon juice, 1 teaspoon = ½ teaspoon vinegar

buttermilk or sour milk, 1 cup = 1 tablespoon lemon juice or vinegar plus milk to make 1 cup (let stand 5 minutes)

whole milk, 1 cup = ½ cup evaporated milk plus ½ cup water or 1 cup reconstituted nonfat dry milk plus 2½ teaspoons butter or margarine

mushrooms, ½ pound = 4 ounces canned mushrooms

mustard, 1 teaspoon dry = 1 tablespoon prepared

onion, 1 small = 1 tablespoon instant minced onion

oregano, 1 teaspoon = 1 teaspoon marjoram

raisins, ½ cup = ½ cup dried cut prunes

shrimp, 1 pound shelled, deveined, cooked = 5 ounces canned shrimp

Tabasco, a few drops = dash of cayenne pepper

tomatoes, 1 cup canned = 1⅓ cup fresh tomatoes simmered 10 minutes

tomato juice, 1 cup = ½ cup tomato sauce plus ½ cup water

Worcestershire, 1 teaspoon = 1 teaspoon bottled steak sauce

yeast, 1 cake compressed = 1 package or 2 teaspoons active dry yeast

EQUIVALENTS AND METRIC CONVERSIONS

LIQUID MEASURE EQUIVALENTS

3 teaspoons = 1 tablespoon

2 tablespoons = 1 fluid ounce

4 tablespoons = ¼ cup = 2 fluid ounces

5 tablespoons + 1 teaspoon = ⅓ cup = 2⅔ ounces

8 tablespoons = ½ cup = 4 fluid ounces

10 tablespoons = 2 teaspoons = ⅔ cup

12 tablespoons = ¾ cup

16 tablespoons = 1 cup = 8 fluid ounces

2 cups = 16 fluid ounces = 1 pint

4 cups = 32 fluid ounces = 1 quart

8 cups = 64 fluid ounces = ½ gallon

4 quarts = 128 fluid ounces = 1 gallon

METRIC CONVERSION TABLE

To change	To	Multiply by
teaspoons	milliliters	5
tablespoons	milliliters	15
fluid ounces	milliliters	30
ounces	grams	28
cups	liters	0.24
pints	liters	0.47
quarts	liters	0.95
gallons	liters	3.8
pounds	kilograms	0.45
Fahrenheit	Celsius	$5/9$ after subtracting 32

MEAT RETAIL CUTS AND
HOW TO COOK THEM

PORK

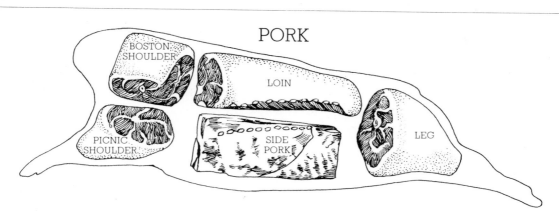

Blade steak
(from the Boston shoulder)
1. Pan-fry
2. Braise

Center loin roast
(from the loin)
1. Roast

Rib chop
(from the loin)
1. Pan-broil
2. Pan-fry
3. Braise

Smoked arm picnic
(from the picnic shoulder)
1. Roast
2. Cook in liquid

Fresh hock
(from the picnic shoulder)
1. Braise
2. Cook in liquid

Spareribs
(from the side pork)
1. Bake
2. Braise
3. Cook in liquid

Slab bacon
(from the side pork)
1. Broil
2. Pan-broil

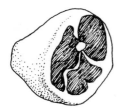

Rump butt portion
(from the leg)
1. Roast
2. Cook in liquid

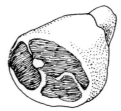

Shank portion
(from the leg)
1. Roast
2. Cook in liquid

Center ham slice
(from the leg)
1. Broil
2. Pan-broil

BEEF

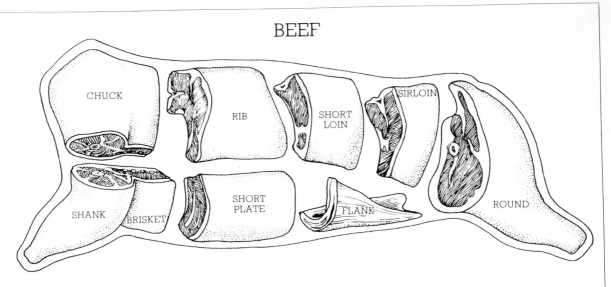

Chuck steak
(from the chuck)
1. Braise
2. Cook in liquid

Blade steak
(from the chuck)
1. Braise
2. Cook in liquid

Arm roast
(from the chuck)
1. Braise
2. Cook in liquid

Rib roast
(from the rib)
1. Roast

Rolled rump roast
(from the round)
1. Braise
2. Cook in liquid

Bottom round roast
(from the round)
1. Braise
2. Cook in liquid

Porterhouse steak
(from the short loin)
1. Broil
2. Pan-broil
3. Grill

T-bone steak
(from the short loin)
1. Broil
2. Pan-broil
3. Grill

Club steak
(from the short loin)
1. Broil
2. Pan-broil
3. Grill

Full-cut round steak
(from the round)
1. Braise
2. Cook in liquid

Shank cross cuts
(from the shank)
1. Braise
2. Cook in liquid

Short ribs
(from the short plate)
1. Braise
2. Cook in liquid

Corned brisket
(from the brisket)
1. Braise
2. Cook in liquid

Flank steak
(from the flank)
1. Broil
2. Braise
3. Grill

Tip roast
(from the round)
1. Braise
2. Cook in liquid

LAMB

Square shoulder
(from the shoulder roast)
1. Roast

Blade chop
(from the shoulder)
1. Broil
2. Pan-broil
3. Pan-fry

Arm chop
(from the shoulder)
1. Broil
2. Pan-broil
3. Pan-fry

Crown roast
(from the rib)
1. Roast

Eight-rib rack
(from the rib)
1. Roast

Loin chops
(from the loin)
1. Broil
2. Pan-broil
3. Pan-fry

Leg, sirloin half
(from the leg)
1. Roast

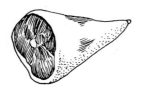

Leg, shank half
(from the leg)
1. Roast

Lamb shank
(from the fore shank)
1. Braise

Breast
(from the breast)
1. Roast
2. Braise

COOKING TEMPERATURES AND TIMES

DEGREES	
	FAHRENHEIT
Low oven	250
Moderate oven	350
Hot oven	400
Broiling	550
Freezing point of water	32
Simmering	180
Boiling	212
Jelly point	220
Soft-ball stage	234–240
Caramel stage	320

BAKING CHART		
MEAT	MINUTES	FAHRENHEIT DEGREES
Beef		
rare	18–20 per lb	300
medium	22–25 per lb	300·
well-done	27–30 per lb	300
Lamb		
pink	15 per lb	325
well-done	30 per lb	300
Pork	40 per lb	350
Veal	30 per lb	325
All rolled roasts	Add 10–15 min per lb	300
Chicken	25	350
Duck	25	350
Fish	20	375

MEAT ROASTING TIME AND TEMPERATURE CHART*

	APPROX. WEIGHT (lbs)	APPROX. COOKING TIME (min per lb)	MEAT THERMOMETER READING (degrees)
BEEF CUT			
Boneless rolled rump	4–6	25–30	150–170
Rib eye	4–6	18–20 20–22 22–24	135 rare 155 medium 170 well-done
Sirloin tip	3½–4	32–40	135–155
Standing rib	4–6	26–32 34–38 40–42	135 rare 155 medium 170 well-done
Tenderloin (425-degree oven)	4–6	45–60 (total cooking time)	135 rare
VEAL CUT			
Leg	5–8	22–32	170
Loin	4–6	22–28	170
Shoulder	4–6	35–45	135–155
PORK CUT			
Boston shoulder	4–6	40–45	170
Crown	4–6	35–40	170
Ham, whole	10–14	18–20	160
Leg, whole, with bone	12–16	22–26	170
Loin roast	3–5	30–35	170
Picnic shoulder	5–8	30–35	170
Tenderloin	½–1	45–60 (total cooking time)	—
LAMB CUT			
Crown	2½–4	30–35 35–40 40–45	140 rare 160 medium 170–180 well-done
Leg, whole, with bone	5–9	20–25 25–30 30–35	140 rare 160 medium 170–180 well-done
Rib	2–3	25–30 30–35 35–40	140 rare 160 medium 170–180 well-done
Shoulder, boneless	3½–5	30–35 35–40 40–45	140 rare 160 medium 170–180 well-done

*Oven temperature is 325 degrees unless specified.

TIMETABLE FOR BROILING STEAKS AND CHOPS

BEEF	THICKNESS	RARE	MEDIUM
Sirloin steak	1 in	20 min	25 min
	1½ in	30 min	35 min
	2 in	40 min	45 min
Porterhouse	Same as sirloin		
Club	1 in	15 min	20 min
	1½ in	25 min	30 min
	2 in	35 min	45 min
Rib	Same as club		

POULTRY ROASTING TIME AND TEMPERATURE CHART

	Approx. Weight (lbs)	Approx. Cooking Time*	Oven Temp.	Meat Thermometer Reading
BIRD				
Frying chicken	3–4	20–25	375	185
Roasting chicken	4–6	20–25	375	185
Rock Cornish game hen	1–1½	45–60	375	—
Turkey breast Half, bone in	2–4	15–20	350	170
Half, boneless	2–4	20–25	350	170
Turkey thigh	½–1½	60	350	185
Turkey hindquarter	2½–4	60	350	185

*To estimate the total cooking time, multiply the weight of the bird by the minutes per pound.

TESTING POULTRY FOR DONENESS

If you are either baking, braising, frying, or sautéing a cut-up chicken, test to see if it is done by cutting a deep slit into the thickest part of the flesh. If the juices run clear yellow, the bird is done; pink blood indicates more cooking time is required. When cooking both thighs and breasts, test the thighs, for they take longer to cook.

The best way to test a roasted chicken for doneness is with a meat thermometer. (The old reliable method of jiggling a leg is not so reliable. It could mean that the dark meat is *over*done.) When the approximate cooking time is nearly over, insert the point of the thermometer into the breast or the thickest part of the thigh. Be careful not to rest it against a bone. The bird is done when the temperature of the breast is 170 degrees and the thigh is 185 degrees.

HOW MUCH IS ENOUGH STUFFING?

When you're roasting chicken, turkey, or game hens, prepare ¾ cup of stuffing per pound of bird. Turkeys that weigh over 14 pounds need only ½ cup of stuffing per pound.

ROASTING CHART FOR WHOLE TURKEY, UNSTUFFED AND COVERED

Weight	Approx. Cooking Time	Oven Temp.
10–14 lb	15 min per lb	325° (185° thermometer)
16–30 lb	12 min per lb	325° (185° thermometer)

ROASTING CHART FOR WHOLE TURKEY, STUFFED AND COVERED

Weight	Approx. Cooking Time	Oven Temp.
4–8 lb	3–4 hr	325°
8–12 lb	4–4½ hr	325°
12–16 lb	4½–5 hr	325°
16–20 lb	5½–7 hr	325°
20–25 lb	7–8½ hr	325°

TESTING FISH FOR DONENESS

Fish can be easily overcooked, and since moistness is crucial for tasty fish, don't wait until it flakes. Stop the cooking process close to the end of the estimated time. Cut a slit in the center of the thickest part of the fish. When the flesh inside is slightly opaque and doesn't look wet, remove it from the heat. The fish will continue to cook by its own internal heat and will flake by the time you are ready to eat it.

PART IV
The Recipe Recordkeeper

HORS D'OEUVRE AND APPETIZERS

Recipe

Source _____   Serves _____

Ingredients _____

_____

_____

_____

_____

Directions _____

_____

_____

_____

_____

_____

_____

_____

_____

_____

_____

_____

_____

Use This Space For Clippings

Recipe

Source _____ Serves _____

Ingredients _____

_____

_____

_____

_____

_____

_____

Directions _____

_____

_____

_____

_____

_____

_____

_____

_____

_____

_____

_____

_____

_____

_____

Recipe

Source _____ Serves _____

Ingredients _____

_____

_____

_____

_____

_____

_____

Directions _____

_____

_____

_____

_____

_____

_____

_____

_____

_____

_____

_____

_____

_____

Recipe

Source _____ Serves _____

Ingredients _____

_____

_____

_____

_____

_____

_____

Directions _____

_____

_____

_____

_____

_____

_____

_____

_____

_____

_____

_____

_____

_____

Use This Space For Clippings

Recipe

Source _____ Serves _____

Ingredients _____

_____

_____

_____

_____

_____

_____

Directions _____

_____

_____

_____

_____

_____

_____

_____

_____

_____

_____

_____

_____

Recipe

Source _____ Serves _____

Ingredients _____

_____

_____

_____

_____

_____

_____

Directions _____

_____

_____

_____

_____

_____

_____

_____

_____

_____

_____

_____

_____

SALADS

Recipe

Source _____ Serves _____

Ingredients _____

_____

_____

_____

_____

Directions _____

_____

_____

_____

_____

_____

_____

_____

_____

_____

_____

_____

_____

_____

_____

Use This Space For Clippings

Recipe

Source _____ Serves _____

Ingredients _____

_____

_____

_____

_____

_____

_____

Directions _____

_____

_____

_____

_____

_____

_____

_____

_____

_____

_____

_____

_____

_____

_____

Recipe

Source _____ Serves _____

Ingredients _____
_____
_____
_____
_____
_____
_____

Directions _____
_____
_____
_____
_____
_____
_____
_____
_____
_____
_____
_____
_____
_____
_____

Use This Space For Clippings

Recipe

Source _____ Serves _____

Ingredients _____

_____

_____

_____

_____

_____

_____

Directions _____

_____

_____

_____

_____

_____

_____

_____

_____

_____

_____

_____

_____

_____

SOUPS AND STOCKS

Recipe

Source _____ Serves _____

Ingredients _____
_____
_____
_____
_____

Directions _____
_____
_____
_____
_____
_____
_____
_____
_____
_____
_____
_____
_____
_____
_____

Use This Space For Clippings

Recipe

Source _____ Serves _____

Ingredients _____

_____

_____

_____

_____

_____

_____

_____

Directions _____

_____

_____

_____

_____

_____

_____

_____

_____

_____

_____

_____

_____

_____

_____

_____

Recipe

Source _____ Serves _____

Ingredients _____

_____

_____

_____

_____

_____

Directions _____

_____

_____

_____

_____

_____

_____

_____

_____

_____

_____

_____

_____

_____

Use This Space For Clippings

Recipe

Source _____ Serves _____

Ingredients _____
_____
_____
_____
_____
_____
_____

Directions _____
_____
_____
_____
_____
_____
_____
_____
_____
_____
_____
_____
_____
_____

PASTA AND RICES

Recipe

Source _____ Serves _____

Ingredients _____

_____

_____

_____

_____

Directions _____

_____

_____

_____

_____

_____

_____

_____

_____

_____

_____

_____

_____

_____

_____

Use This Space For Clippings

Recipe

Source _____ Serves _____

Ingredients _____

_____

_____

_____

_____

_____

_____

Directions _____

_____

_____

_____

_____

_____

_____

_____

_____

_____

_____

_____

_____

_____

_____

Recipe

Source _____ Serves _____

Ingredients _____

_____

_____

_____

_____

_____

_____

Directions _____

_____

_____

_____

_____

_____

_____

_____

_____

_____

_____

_____

_____

Use This Space For Clippings

Recipe

Source _____ Serves _____

Ingredients _____
_____
_____
_____
_____
_____
_____

Directions _____
_____
_____
_____
_____
_____
_____
_____
_____
_____
_____
_____
_____
_____
_____

EGGS

Recipe

Source _____ Serves _____

Ingredients _____

_____

_____

_____

_____

Directions _____

_____

_____

_____

_____

_____

_____

_____

_____

_____

_____

_____

_____

_____

_____

_____

Use This Space For Clippings

Recipe

Source _____ Serves _____

Ingredients _____

_____

_____

_____

_____

_____

_____

Directions _____

_____

_____

_____

_____

_____

_____

_____

_____

_____

_____

_____

_____

_____

_____

_____

Recipe

Source _____ Serves _____

Ingredients _____

_____

_____

_____

_____

_____

_____

Directions _____

_____

_____

_____

_____

_____

_____

_____

_____

_____

_____

_____

_____

_____

_____

VEGETABLES

Recipe _____

Source _____ Serves _____

Ingredients _____
_____
_____
_____
_____

Directions _____
_____
_____
_____
_____
_____
_____
_____
_____
_____
_____
_____
_____
_____
_____
_____

Use This Space For Clippings

Recipe

Source _____ Serves _____

Ingredients _____

_____

_____

_____

_____

_____

_____

Directions _____

_____

_____

_____

_____

_____

_____

_____

_____

_____

_____

_____

_____

_____

Recipe

Source _____ Serves _____

Ingredients _____

_____

_____

_____

_____

_____

_____

Directions _____

_____

_____

_____

_____

_____

_____

_____

_____

_____

_____

_____

_____

_____

_____

Use This Space For Clippings

Recipe

Source

Serves

Ingredients

Directions

SAUCES, DRESSINGS, AND STUFFINGS

Recipe

Source _____ Serves _____

Ingredients _____

_____

_____

_____

_____

Directions _____

_____

_____

_____

_____

_____

_____

_____

_____

_____

_____

_____

_____

_____

_____

Use This Space For Clippings

Recipe

Source _____ Serves _____

Ingredients _____

_____

_____

_____

_____

_____

_____

Directions _____

_____

_____

_____

_____

_____

_____

_____

_____

_____

_____

_____

_____

_____

Recipe

Source _____ Serves _____

Ingredients _____

_____

_____

_____

_____

_____

_____

Directions _____

_____

_____

_____

_____

_____

_____

_____

_____

_____

_____

_____

_____

Use This Space For Clippings

Recipe

Source _____ Serves _____

Ingredients _____

_____

_____

_____

_____

_____

_____

Directions _____

_____

_____

_____

_____

_____

_____

_____

_____

_____

_____

_____

_____

_____

_____

FISH

Recipe

Source _____ Serves _____

Ingredients _____

_____

_____

_____

_____

Directions _____

_____

_____

_____

_____

_____

_____

_____

_____

_____

_____

_____

_____

_____

Use This Space For Clippings

Recipe

Source _____ Serves _____

Ingredients _____

_____

_____

_____

_____

_____

_____

Directions _____

_____

_____

_____

_____

_____

_____

_____

_____

_____

_____

_____

_____

_____

Recipe

Source _____ Serves _____

Ingredients _____

_____

_____

_____

_____

_____

Directions _____

_____

_____

_____

_____

_____

_____

_____

_____

_____

_____

_____

_____

Use This Space For Clippings

Recipe

Source_____ Serves_____

Ingredients_____

_____

_____

_____

_____

_____

_____

Directions_____

_____

_____

_____

_____

_____

_____

_____

_____

_____

_____

_____

_____

_____

POULTRY AND GAMEBIRDS

Recipe

Source _____ Serves _____

Ingredients _____

_____

_____

_____

_____

Directions _____

_____

_____

_____

_____

_____

_____

_____

_____

_____

_____

_____

_____

_____

_____

Use This Space For Clippings

Recipe

Source _____ Serves _____

Ingredients _____

_____

_____

_____

_____

_____

_____

Directions _____

_____

_____

_____

_____

_____

_____

_____

_____

_____

_____

_____

_____

_____

Recipe

Source _____ Serves _____

Ingredients _____
_____
_____
_____
_____
_____
_____

Directions _____
_____
_____
_____
_____
_____
_____
_____
_____
_____
_____
_____
_____
_____
_____
_____
_____
_____

Use This Space For Clippings

Recipe

Source_____ Serves_____

Ingredients_____

_____

_____

_____

_____

_____

_____

Directions_____

_____

_____

_____

_____

_____

_____

_____

_____

_____

_____

_____

_____

_____

_____

Recipe

Source _____ Serves _____

Ingredients _____

_____

_____

_____

_____

_____

_____

Directions _____

_____

_____

_____

_____

_____

_____

_____

_____

_____

_____

_____

_____

_____

Use This Space For Clippings

MEAT

Recipe _____

Source _____ Serves _____

Ingredients _____

_____

_____

_____

_____

Directions _____

_____

_____

_____

_____

_____

_____

_____

_____

_____

_____

_____

_____

_____

Use This Space For Clippings

Recipe

Source _____ Serves _____

Ingredients _____

_____
_____
_____
_____
_____
_____

Directions _____

_____
_____
_____
_____
_____
_____
_____
_____
_____
_____
_____
_____
_____
_____

Recipe

Source

Serves

Ingredients

Directions

Use This Space For Clippings

Recipe

Source

Serves

Ingredients

Directions

Recipe _____

Source _____ Serves _____

Ingredients _____

_____
_____
_____
_____
_____
_____

Directions _____

_____
_____
_____
_____
_____
_____
_____
_____
_____
_____
_____
_____
_____
_____
_____
_____

Recipe

Source _____ Serves _____

Ingredients _____

_____

_____

_____

_____

_____

_____

Directions _____

_____

_____

_____

_____

_____

_____

_____

_____

_____

_____

_____

_____

_____

_____

_____

Use This Space For Clippings

Recipe _____

Source _____ Serves _____

Ingredients _____

_____

_____

_____

_____

_____

Directions _____

_____

_____

_____

_____

_____

_____

_____

_____

_____

_____

_____

_____

BREADS

Recipe _____

Source _____ Serves _____

Ingredients _____

_____

_____

_____

_____

Directions _____

_____

_____

_____

_____

_____

_____

_____

_____

_____

_____

_____

_____

_____

_____

_____

_____

Use This Space For Clippings

Recipe

Source _____ Serves _____

Ingredients _____

_____

_____

_____

_____

_____

_____

Directions _____

_____

_____

_____

_____

_____

_____

_____

_____

_____

_____

_____

_____

_____

_____

_____

Recipe

Source _____ Serves _____

Ingredients _____

_____
_____
_____
_____
_____

Directions _____

_____
_____
_____
_____
_____
_____
_____
_____
_____
_____
_____
_____
_____

Recipe

Source _____ Serves _____

Ingredients _____

_____

_____

_____

_____

_____

_____

Directions _____

_____

_____

_____

_____

_____

_____

_____

_____

_____

_____

_____

_____

_____

_____

_____

Use This Space For Clippings

PIES, PASTRIES, CAKES, AND COOKIES

Recipe

Source _____ Serves _____

Ingredients _____

_____

_____

_____

_____

Directions _____

_____

_____

_____

_____

_____

_____

_____

_____

_____

_____

_____

_____

_____

_____

Use This Space For Clippings

Recipe

Source_____ Serves_____

Ingredients_____

_____

_____

_____

_____

_____

_____

Directions_____

_____

_____

_____

_____

_____

_____

_____

_____

_____

_____

_____

_____

_____

_____

_____

Recipe

Source _____ Serves _____

Ingredients _____
_____
_____
_____
_____
_____
_____

Directions _____
_____
_____
_____
_____
_____
_____
_____
_____
_____
_____
_____
_____
_____
_____

Use This Space For Clippings

Recipe

Source _____ Serves _____

Ingredients _____

_____

_____

_____

_____

_____

Directions _____

_____

_____

_____

_____

_____

_____

_____

_____

_____

_____

_____

_____

Recipe

Source _____ Serves _____

Ingredients _____

_____

_____

_____

_____

_____

_____

Directions _____

_____

_____

_____

_____

_____

_____

_____

_____

_____

_____

_____

_____

Use This Space For Clippings

ICINGS, CANDIES, TOPPINGS, AND GLAZES

Recipe

Source _____ Serves _____

Ingredients _____

_____

_____

_____

_____

Directions _____

_____

_____

_____

_____

_____

_____

_____

_____

_____

_____

_____

_____

_____

_____

_____

Use This Space For Clippings

Recipe

Source _____ Serves _____

Ingredients _____

_____

_____

_____

_____

_____

_____

Directions _____

_____

_____

_____

_____

_____

_____

_____

_____

_____

_____

_____

_____

_____

_____

Recipe

Source _____ Serves _____

Ingredients _____

Directions _____

PUDDINGS, MOUSSES, AND FRUITS

Recipe

Source _____ Serves _____

Ingredients _____

_____

_____

_____

_____

Directions _____

_____

_____

_____

_____

_____

_____

_____

_____

_____

_____

_____

_____

_____

_____

Use This Space For Clippings

Recipe

Source _____ Serves _____

Ingredients _____

_____

_____

_____

_____

_____

_____

Directions _____

_____

_____

_____

_____

_____

_____

_____

_____

_____

_____

_____

_____

_____

Use This Space For Clippings

JELLIES AND PRESERVES

Recipe

Source _____ Serves _____

Ingredients _____

_____

_____

_____

_____

Directions _____

_____

_____

_____

_____

_____

_____

_____

_____

_____

_____

_____

_____

Use This Space For Clippings

Use This Space For Clippings

Recipe

Source _____ Serves _____

Ingredients _____
_____
_____
_____
_____
_____
_____
_____

Directions _____
_____
_____
_____
_____
_____
_____
_____
_____
_____
_____
_____
_____
_____
_____

PICKLES AND RELISHES

Recipe

Source _____ Serves _____

Ingredients _____

_____

_____

_____

_____

Directions _____

_____

_____

_____

_____

_____

_____

_____

_____

_____

_____

_____

_____

_____

Use This Space For Clippings

Use This Space For Clippings

Recipe

Source _____ Serves _____

Ingredients _____

Directions _____

BEVERAGES

Recipe _____

Source _____ Serves _____

Ingredients _____
_____
_____
_____
_____

Directions _____
_____
_____
_____
_____
_____
_____
_____
_____
_____
_____
_____
_____
_____
_____

Use This Space For Clippings

Use This Space For Clippings

Recipe

Source _____ Serves _____

Ingredients _____

_____

_____

_____

_____

_____

_____

Directions _____

_____

_____

_____

_____

_____

_____

_____

_____

_____

_____

_____

_____

_____

Recipe

Source _____ Serves _____

Ingredients _____
_____
_____
_____
_____
_____

Directions _____
_____
_____
_____
_____
_____
_____
_____
_____
_____
_____
_____
_____
_____